CC

M000191749

INTRODUCTION

The Apostles is a collection of the catecheses Pope Benedict XVI gave during his weekly General Audiences in 2006 and 2007. The talks were given in either St. Peter's Square or, in less favorable weather, the Paul VI Hall next to St. Peter's Basilica.

Pope Benedict has followed the tradition of John Paul II in organizing the General Audience talks according to themes and using them as an opportunity for a systematic teaching. Pope John Paul II's formulation of the "Theology of the Body," for example, was publicly articulated in General Audience talks from 1979 to 1984.

This teaching is rich in scriptural, historical, and theological content. In each presentation, the Pope takes care to indicate contemporary spiritual applications of each of his points — applications that are helpful to our faith as individuals and our lives as members of the Body of Christ, the Church.

This study guide is offered to help readers of *The Apostles* deepen their understanding of the content offered and reflect on the contemporary applications. The major themes that readers and participants will encounter include:

- Who is Jesus and what was His mission on earth?
- How is His mission continued today?
- Is it really possible to know Jesus today? How?
- What is an Apostle?
- What were the Apostles' faith and mission all about?
- What is the relationship between Jesus, the Apostles, and the Church today?
- What do each of the Apostles, in their journey with Jesus and their missions after Pentecost, reveal to us about our

own lives as disciples of Jesus and members of His Body, the Church?

- How do the struggles and joys of the Apostles shed light on our own? How can we be strengthened in our role as disciples to invite people to "come and see" Jesus?

HINTS FOR LEADING AN EFFECTIVE GROUP STUDY OF *THE APOSTLES*

1. The group leader should have a clear sense of the purpose of the gatherings. *The Apostles* and this study guide are designed to help readers and participants grow in their understanding of the *content* and *nature* of faith in Jesus Christ as witnessed to and handed down by the Apostles, and to apply that understanding to their lives today as individuals and as a Church.

This distinguishes this offering from a "faith-sharing" model in which the emphasis is on participants sharing their stories and feelings about a topic and reacting to each others' stories. There is a place for the faith-sharing model in adult catechesis. However, *The Apostles* is not designed with that goal in mind, but rather to feed the hunger many adults have to grow in understanding of the *content* of faith in Jesus Christ and how to experience that today, in their own lives as Catholics. The Pope is primarily a teacher, and participants will have gathered to learn from him.

2. The group leader should be a person who can effectively facilitate learning through discussion. That person should have the following qualities:

- The commitment to prepare beforehand, have a clear sense of the points to be covered, and introduce each session with a summary of the chapter to be discussed.
- A balance of openness, flexibility, confidence, and firmness. The group leader should have a welcoming person-

ality so that all participants feel encouraged to speak. He or she must also have the confidence to respectfully end discussions that have gone off-course and to redirect those discussions. Allowing one person to dominate a session is unfair to the other participants, and a group leader must keep this in mind and be sensitive to it.

- The willingness to say, "I don't know the answer to that question. Let me look it up for the next time," and move on.

3. Problems can sometimes arise in group discussions. Be aware, in particular, of the following:

- Dominant personalities: The best way to deal with dominant personalities in a discussion is to consciously and frequently encourage others to speak. If the problem persists, the individual who is presenting the problem can be spoken to privately.
- Too much information: Occasionally, individuals will use a group setting to unload personal problems or issues with the Church in ways inappropriate to the setting. When this happens, a group leader should respectfully but firmly redirect the discussion, giving due credit to the individual's pain. Afterwards, depending on the nature of the individual's issue, the group leader should suggest that the person contact a priest or perhaps even alert a priest about the situation himself. Again, the leader's primary responsibility is to the group as a whole.
- Quiet personalities: Individuals who don't participate can be gently encouraged to speak, but not persistently. If a person is content to listen and learn, let them do that — do not draw attention to them in a joking manner.
- Going off topic: Sometimes this is serendipitous, sometimes it is a problem. The group leader should be sensitive

to this, careful to judge whether the course of a discussion is actually helpful to everyone present (is everyone engaged and interested?) or if it is just serving as a means for a small part of the group to engage with each other. If it is the latter, the discussion should be brought back to the topic. Participants' time is valuable, and their sacrifice to be present at the session should be respected.

PRACTICAL POINTERS

Place: It is best to have parish-sponsored events on the parish grounds.

Size: It is very difficult to have a group *discussion* with more than 15-20 people. If you have more than that register, consider breaking the group in two, adding a session, or even formatting the sessions along the lines of a class rather than a discussion.

Time: Evenings, in between Masses on Sunday mornings, weekday mornings, during children's religious education sessions, or on weekday mornings after children are dropped off at the parish school are all good times for adult education in a parish. Different times appeal to different groups of people, which is why, if possible, it is good to try to have multiple sessions. Some older people, for example, don't like coming out at night, and people who work during the day prefer weekend or evening times. At least one session should have child care provided, free of charge, so that younger parents may attend.

Materials: All participants should have a copy of *The Apostles*, this study guide, and, ideally, a Bible. If possible, participants should not be charged for materials, as this is immediately discouraging to some potential participants. Free-will offerings might be taken, but individually paying for the materials should not be a requirement or expectation for participation. Parishes might also consider making the materials available for those who cannot participate in the group study.

Number and length of sessions: There are 12 sessions in the study guide, but leaders should feel free to design their own program and be flexible. No sessions should be omitted, for everything Pope Benedict says in these talks is interrelated and his ideas build on each other. But leaders might find that some topics lend themselves to more than one session (for example, the material on Paul and John is particularly rich and diverse). The introductory chapters have been broken up into two sections, one at the beginning, and one at the end, with the thought that chapters three and four would provide a good opportunity for wrapping up the entire series.

Ideally the 12 sessions have been designed in such a way that they could be done in two series of six sessions, for example one six-week session in the Fall and another six-week session in the Spring.

Sessions should be planned to be from 60 to 90 minutes in length, with time for a break and simple refreshments such as water and coffee. Whatever the planned length, stick to it out of respect for participants' busy lives and varied commitments.

USING THE STUDY GUIDE

All of the materials presented in the study guide are intended to support a helpful and enriching session. Leaders may use as many questions from either category as desired as well as add their own. Prayers are designed to help enhance the catechetical experience – they are drawn from the rich, living tradition of the Church and are all related to the topic of each session.

PLANNING YOUR SESSION

Begin the session with the *Sign of the Cross* and the *Prayer to the Holy Spirit*:

Sign of the Cross
In the Name of the Father, the Son, and the Holy Spirit. Amen

Prayer to the Holy Spirit
V. *Come, Holy Spirit, fill the hearts of Your faithful and kindle in us the fire of Your love.*

R. *Send forth Your Spirit and we shall be created, and You will renew the face of the earth.*

Let us pray: O God, who by the light of the Holy Spirit instructs the hearts of the faithful, grant that by that same Spirit we may be ever wise and rejoice in His consolations. We make our prayer through Christ, our Lord. Amen.

Reading
Invite a participant to read aloud the excerpted passage from *The Apostles* given at the beginning of each set of questions. Then allow for a few moments of quiet recollection and reflection on passage from *The Apostles* (about five minutes).

Discussion
Begin the discussion with a starter question. For example, for the first session:

"What is your general impression, from reading these two chapters, of the importance of the Apostles in the Church?"

Use the response as a brief opportunity to help participants become comfortable and then move into whatever Questions for

Study and Questions for Reflection you have decided to use to guide the discussion.

Spend most of the time on the Questions for Study, using the last fifteen minutes of the session for the Questions for Reflection.

Closing Prayer

Make the closing prayer simple. Have a participant read the suggested Scripture passage, pause for a moment, and then invite participants to pray the Lord's Prayer, perhaps with these words:

Leader: "*Let us now pray together the prayer Jesus taught the Apostles.*"
All: *Our Father . . .*

End with an intercessory prayer to the Apostle or Apostles who were the focus of the session:

Leader: *Most Holy Apostles <u>insert name(s)</u>*
Group: *Pray for us*

All make the *Sign of the Cross.*

Chosen by Jesus

Jesus of Nazareth and the Twelve Apostles

(Chapters One to Two)

Begin the session with the *Sign of the Cross* and the *Prayer to the Holy Spirit* (see page 10).

Excerpt from *The Apostles*:

"Communion" is truly the Good News, the remedy given to us by the Lord to fight the loneliness that threatens everyone today, the precious gift that makes us feel welcomed and beloved by God, in the unity of his People gathered in the name of the Trinity; it is the light that makes the Church shine forth like a beacon raised among the peoples. (page 22)

Quiet Reflection

NOTES

QUESTIONS FOR DISCUSSION

Questions for Study

1. "Through the Apostles, we come to Jesus himself" (page 9). What does this mean?

2. What is the significance of the number twelve in terms of the Apostles?

3. What is the relationship between Jesus, the Eucharist, the Apostles, and the Church?

4. At what point does Jesus' call to the future Apostles come in his ministry? What does this signify about their role?

5. What role does the Apostles' relationship with Jesus play in their identity and mission as Apostles?

6. Why is Jesus' "gathering together" the lost sheep of Israel a prophetic sign?

7. Pope Benedict describes the essence of the Church as "communion."

   • What is the source of communion in the Church? How does it come about?

   • What are the two dimensions of communion for members of the Church?

   • "'Communion' is truly the Good News . . ." (page 22). Why is this so?

8. Given the centrality and understanding of communion, what, then, is the Church?

9. What is the ministry of the Apostles all about, particularly in relationship to communion?

10. What is the relationship of the ministry of the Apostles to truth?

11. What is the relationship between truth and love?

Questions for Reflection

1. How is "communion" different from "community"?

2. Reflect on the links between your life as a Catholic today and the apostolic Church. How have you experienced the presence of Jesus in the sacramental and spiritual life of the Church today?

3. Why is "this individualistically chosen Jesus . . . an imaginary Jesus" (page 12)? What are the risks in thinking that we can know Jesus apart from the ancient communion that is the Church?

4. How do the insights of this chapter impact your understanding of Eucharist?

NOTES

CLOSING PRAYER

Scripture Reading

So then you are no longer strangers and sojourners, but you are fellow citizens with the saints and members of the household of God, built upon the foundation of the apostles and prophets, Christ Jesus himself being the cornerstone, in whom the whole structure is joined together and grows into a holy temple in the Lord; in whom you also are built into it for a dwelling place of God in the Spirit. (Ephesians 2:19-22)

Briefly pause.

Lord's Prayer

Leader: *Most Holy Apostles*
Group: *Pray for us*

All make the *Sign of the Cross.*

Peter

(Chapter Five)

Begin the session with the *Sign of the Cross* and the *Prayer to the Holy Spirit* (see page 10).

Excerpt from *The Apostles*:

Peter could not yet imagine that one day he would arrive in Rome and that here he would be a "fisher of men" for the Lord. He accepted this surprising call, he let himself be involved in this great adventure: he was generous; he recognized his limits but believed in the one who was calling him and followed the dream of his heart. He said "yes," a courageous and generous "yes," and became a disciple of Jesus. (page 47)

Quiet Reflection

NOTES

QUESTIONS FOR DISCUSSION

Questions for Study

1. What was Peter's family and religious background? How would you describe his character?

2. "The boat of Peter becomes the chair of Jesus" (page 47). What does this mean?

3. The first stage of Peter's faith journey was his answer to Jesus' call. How did he answer?

4. The second stage of Peter's journey is represented by his answer to Jesus' question at Caesarea Philippi. What happened here? What was the challenge to Peter's faith? What did he need to understand?

5. How does the multiplication of the loaves reinforce the truth that Jesus revealed to Peter at Caesarea Philippi?

6. In what sense does Peter's denial of Jesus and his confession make him "ready for his mission"?

7. What does the post-Resurrection conversation of Jesus and Peter reveal about Jesus' presence in our lives and what he expects of us?

8. What is unusual about Peter's new name? What does it mean?

9. What are some of the signs of Peter's special prominence among the Apostles that we read about in the Gospels?

10. What images in the Gospel express the term "primacy of jurisdiction"? What does it mean?

Questions for Reflection

1. Pope Benedict describes what Peter was answering as a call to be involved in a "great adventure." How have you experienced the Christian life as a "great adventure"? How can you better convey this experience of the Christian life to others?

2. What does it mean to answer the call of Jesus, with a "courageous and generous 'yes'"? In what ways has your "yes" been courageous and generous? It what ways has it not?

3. Peter discovered that Jesus' way of being the Messiah was not what he expected. What temptations to "go before Jesus" rather than follow him have you expected? How has God surprised you in defying your expectations?

4. "The school of faith is not a triumphal march but a journey marked daily by suffering and love, trials and faithfulness" (page 52). How have you experienced this in your own life?

5. What happens to us in our faith lives if we do not learn from Peter and accept our own fragility and weakness?

6. In what way is Peter's role among the Apostles a gift to us today? What does it protect?

NOTES

CLOSING PRAYER

Scripture Reading

When they had finished breakfast, Jesus said to Simon Peter, "Simon, son of John, do you love me more than these?" He said to him, "Yes, Lord; you know that I love you." He said to him, "Feed my lambs." A second time he said to him, "Simon, son of John, do you love me?" He said to him, "Yes, Lord; you know that I love you." He said to him, "Tend my sheep." He said to him the third time, "Simon, son of John, do you love me?" Peter was grieved because he said to him the third time, "Do you love me?" And he said to him, "Lord, you know everything; you know that I love you." Jesus said to him, "Feed my sheep. Truly, truly, I say to you, when you were young, you girded yourself and walked where you would; but when you are old, you will stretch out your hands, and another will gird you and carry you where you do not wish to go." (This he said to show by what death he was to glorify God.) And after this he said to him, "Follow me." (John 21:15-19)

Briefly pause.

Lord's Prayer

Leader: *St. Peter*
Group: *Pray for us*

All make the *Sign of the Cross.*

Andrew, James the Greater, and James the Lesser

(Chapters Six to Eight)

Begin the session with the *Sign of the Cross* and the *Prayer to the Holy Spirit* (see page 10).

Excerpt from *The Apostles*:

The Apostle Andrew, therefore, teaches us to follow Jesus with promptness, to speak enthusiastically about him to those we meet, and especially, to cultivate a relationship of true familiarity with him, acutely aware that in him alone can we find the ultimate meaning of our life and death. (page 64)

Quiet Reflection

NOTES

QUESTIONS FOR DISCUSSION

Questions for Study

1. What do we know about Andrew's life before he met Jesus?
2. Why is Andrew called *Protokletos?*
3. What are the three occasions, after his initial call, in which Andrew is mentioned in the Gospels?
4. How does tradition describe Andrew's death? How is it similar to Peter's?
5. At what two important events was James the Greater present? How are these events related?
6. When did James die? In what circumstances?
7. Who was James the Lesser?
8. What role did James play in the struggles of the early Church? What did the result of those early struggles mean for Christianity?
9. What is the main focus and theme of the Letter of James?

Questions for Reflection

1. The Gospels record Andrew asking questions of Jesus. What role does asking questions of the Lord, like Andrew did, play in your spiritual life? How do you discern His answers? What role does the presence of Jesus in the Church – in the sacramental life, spiritual traditions, Scripture, and Church teaching – play in your discernment?
2. Andrew spoke "enthusiastically" about Jesus to others. Are you comfortable speaking about your faith in Jesus to others? What would help you be more like Andrew?
3. An ancient story describes Andrew as welcoming the cross upon which he would die. What does this mean to you? How has the Cross of Jesus helped you find meaning in suffering?

4. James left the "boat" of his own secure life to follow Jesus. What boats have you left for the sake of following Jesus? Why is it hard to leave the boat? What are the rewards?

5. Who are some people you have known or known about who exemplify the unity of faith and charity James emphasizes in his letter? What characterizes their lives?

6. How can you balance the human need to plan our lives with an openness to the will of God? What does that mean in practical, everyday terms to you?

NOTES

CLOSING PRAYER

Scripture Reading

Then the mother of the sons of Zebedee came up to him, with her sons, and kneeling before him she asked him for something. And he said to her, "What do you want?" She said to him, "Command that these two sons of mine may sit, one at your right hand and one at your left, in your kingdom." But Jesus answered, "You do not know what you are asking. Are you able to drink the cup that I am to drink?" They said to him, "We are able." He said to them, "You will drink my cup, but to sit at my right hand and at my left is not mine to grant, but it is for those for whom it has been prepared by my Father." And when the ten heard it, they were indignant at the two brothers. But Jesus called them to him and said, "You know that the rulers of the Gentiles lord it over them, and their great men exercise authority over them. It shall not be so among you; but whoever would be great among you must be your servant, and whoever would be first among you must be your slave; even as the Son of man came not to be served but to serve, and to give his life as a ransom for many." (Matthew 20:20-28)

Briefly pause.

Lord's Prayer

Leader: *Sts. Andrew, James, and James*
Group: *Pray for us*

All make the *Sign of the Cross*.

SESSION 4

John

(Chapter Nine)

OPENING PRAYER AND READING

Begin the session with the *Sign of the Cross* and the *Prayer to the Holy Spirit* (see page 10).

Excerpt from **The Apostles**:

May the Lord help us to study at John's school and learn the great lesson of love, so as to feel we are loved by Christ "to the end," and spend our lives for him. (page 79)

Quiet Reflection

```
                        NOTES




```

26

QUESTIONS FOR DISCUSSION

Questions for Study

1. What does John teach us about being a disciple? What characterizes the relationship of a disciple to Jesus?
2. What are the three components of the Christian understanding of love?
3. What is radical and new about the Christian proclamation that "God is love"?
4. How has God expressed his love for human beings?
5. How does Jesus' love for us reach us?
6. What is the uniqueness of Christian love?
7. What is the context and audience of the Apocalypse of John?
8. What is the meaning and power of the image of the Lamb in the Apocalypse?
9. What is the meaning of the scroll in the Apocalypse? What does it tell us about human events and the history of the world?
10. Why, in the Christian view, is suffering a "paradox"?

Questions for Reflection

1. John, a follower of Jesus, has a relationship of close friendship with him. What role does your friendship with Jesus play in your life? How do you strengthen your friendship with Jesus through his Presence in the sacramental and spiritual life of the Church?
2. The Apostles' journey with Jesus was not just physical, but an "interior" journey. What have you learned on your journey with Jesus so far in your life? How has this journey changed you?
3. Pope Benedict writes that "... each one of us, always and over and over again, must ask himself or herself..." what the proper response to Jesus' outpouring of love is. What is

the response in your heart? How do you express this response?

4. Why might the command of Jesus to love as he has loved us, "invite and disturb us"?

5. How does trust in God help you make sense of what seems senseless? How does the Christian understanding of suffering differ from that of the world?

6. What hope can you derive from the message of John's Apocalypse?

7. When you pray, "Come Lord Jesus," what is your hope?

NOTES

CLOSING PRAYER

Scripture Reading

"This is my commandment, that you love one another as I have loved you. Greater love has no man than this, that a man lay down his life for his friends. You are my friends if you do what I command you. No longer do I call you servants, for the servant does not know what his master is doing; but I have called you friends, for all that I have heard from my Father I have made known to you. You did not choose me, but I chose you and appointed you that you should go and bear fruit and that your fruit should abide; so that whatever you ask the Father in my name, he may give it to you. This I command you, to love one another." (John 15:12-17)

Briefly pause.

Lord's Prayer

Leader: *St. John*
Group: *Pray for us*

All make the *Sign of the Cross.*

Matthew, Philip, Thomas, and Bartholomew

(Chapters Ten to Thirteen)

OPENING PRAYER AND READING

Begin the session with the *Sign of the Cross* and the *Prayer to the Holy Spirit* (see page 10).

Excerpt from *The Apostles*:

Closeness, familiarity and habit make us discover the true identity of Jesus Christ. The Apostle Philip reminds us precisely of this. And thus he invites us to "come" and "see," that is, to enter into contact by listening, responding and communion of life with Jesus, day by day. (page 96)

Quiet Reflection

NOTES

QUESTIONS FOR DISCUSSION

Questions for Study

1. What was Matthew's background? What can we deduce about his life from the Gospels?
2. Why were tax collectors seen as "public sinners" during the time of Jesus?
3. What "paradox" does Matthew's call reveal?
4. What was it that Matthew left behind?
5. What did ancient writers suggest about Matthew and the Gospel that bears his name?
6. Who was Philip? What was his relationship to other Apostles?
7. What does Philip's invitation to "come and see" reveal to us about discipleship and evangelization? What is it we are doing when we evangelize?
8. What is the life of a disciple all about? How does a disciple relate to Jesus?
9. What does Philip ask Jesus at the Last Supper? What is Jesus' response? What do they reveal about Jesus?
10. What do we know about Thomas?
11. What questions did Thomas ask of Jesus? What do these tell us about our relationship to Jesus?
12. What does Thomas' encounter with Jesus after the Resurrection reveal about how Jesus is recognized now?
13. What do we know about Bartholomew?
14. Why did Nathanael (identified with Bartholomew) follow Jesus?

Questions for Reflection

1. How does Matthew's call challenge you in the way you see others?
2. In what aspects of the Church's life do you see Jesus' invitation to Matthew, the public sinner, lived out today?

3. What have you, like Matthew, left behind? What do you still cling to? What might help someone leave behind sinful activities in order to follow Jesus?
4. When we invite others to "come and see" today, what aspects of Church life are we inviting them to come and see to encounter Jesus?
5. What role does the sacramental life of the Church play in your "sharing in the life of Jesus" as a disciple?
6. "If we truly want to know the Face of God, all we have to do is to contemplate the Face of Jesus!" (page 99). What do you learn about God when you contemplate the Face of Jesus? What does it mean to be tempted to simply "look into the mirror" instead?
7. What does it mean to you to know that Jesus is recognized by his wounds? Where do you see Jesus wounded?

NOTES

CLOSING PRAYER

Scripture Reading

Now Philip was from Bethsaida, the city of Andrew and Peter. Philip found Nathanael, and said to him, "We have found him of whom Moses in the law and also the prophets wrote, Jesus of Nazareth, the son of Joseph." Nathanael said to him, "Can anything good come out of Nazareth?" Philip said to him, "Come and see." (John 1:44-46)

Lord's Prayer

Briefly pause.

Leader: *Sts. Matthew, Philip, Thomas, and Bartholomew*
Group: *Pray for us*

All make the *Sign of the Cross.*

Simon and Jude

(Chapter Fourteen)

Begin the session with the *Sign of the Cross* and the *Prayer to the Holy Spirit* (see page 10).

Excerpt from *The Apostles*:

> *It was people who interested him, not social classes or labels! And the best thing is that in the group of his followers, despite their differences, they all lived side by side, overcoming imaginable difficulties: indeed, what bound them together was Jesus himself, in whom they all found themselves united with one another. (page 112)*

Quiet Reflection

NOTES

QUESTIONS FOR DISCUSSION

Questions for Study

1. What do we know about Simon and Jude?
2. Who were the "Zealots"?
3. What does Jesus' inclusion of both Matthew and Simon reveal about the nature of the community of the Apostles? What binds them together?
4. What are the "Catholic Letters" in the New Testament?
5. What is the focus of the Letter of Jude? What are his concerns about the Church?

Questions for Reflection

1. How have you experienced the diversity of the Church? How have you experienced communion (the union brought about by God) and Communion (the Eucharist) in the midst of this diversity?
2. Do you ever yearn for God to make his presence known more obviously? What helps you understand Jesus' words to Simon more deeply in terms of your own life?
3. What conflicts have you experienced between the values of the world and the values of the Gospel? What does the presence of Jesus in the Church offer you to help you resolve these conflicts?

NOTES

CLOSING PRAYER

Scripture Reading

But you, beloved, build yourselves up on your most holy faith; pray in the Holy Spirit; keep yourselves in the love of God; wait for the mercy of our Lord Jesus Christ unto eternal life. And convince some, who doubt; save some, by snatching them out of the fire; on some have mercy with fear, hating even the garment spotted by the flesh. Now to him who is able to keep you from falling and to present you without blemish before the presence of his glory with rejoicing, to the only God, our Savior through Jesus Christ our Lord, be glory, majesty, dominion, and authority, before all time and now and for ever. Amen. (Jude 20-25)

Briefly pause.

Lord's Prayer

Leader: *Sts. Simon and Jude*
Group: *Pray for us*

All make the *Sign of the Cross.*

The Living Body of Christ

Judas Iscariot and Matthias

(Chapter Fifteen)

Begin the session with the *Sign of the Cross* and the *Prayer to the Holy Spirit* (see page 10).

Excerpt from *The Apostles*:

The possibilities to pervert the human heart are truly many. The only way to prevent it consists in not cultivating an individualistic, autonomous vision of things, but on the contrary, by putting oneself always on the side of Jesus, assuming his point of view. We must daily seek to build full communion with him. (page 120)

Quiet Reflection

NOTES

QUESTIONS FOR DISCUSSION

Questions for Study

1. How is Judas described in the gospels before his betrayal of Jesus?
2. Why did Judas betray Jesus?
3. What was the difference between Peter's repentance and that of Judas?
4. What are the two points about Jesus that we can draw from the example of Judas?
5. Who was Matthias?

Questions for Reflection

1. Do you ever experience your own motivations as a mystery? What gives you strength to move beyond your sin and repent?
2. What does it mean to you to know that Jesus respects your freedom? Does this mean everything you might choose is acceptable? How do you discern the ways to use your freedom as a disciple of Jesus?
3. How does the presence of "traitorous Christians in the Church" impact your sense of your own responsibilities?

NOTES

CLOSING PRAYER

Scripture Reading

In those days Peter stood up among the brethren (the company of persons was in all about a hundred and twenty), and said, "Brethren, the scripture had to be fulfilled, which the Holy Spirit spoke beforehand by the mouth of David, concerning Judas who was guide to those who arrested Jesus. For he was numbered among us, and was allotted his share in this ministry. (Now this man bought a field with the reward of his wickedness; and falling headlong he burst open in the middle and all his bowels gushed out. And it became known to all the inhabitants of Jerusalem, so that the field was called in their language Akeldama, that is, Field of Blood.) For it is written in the book of Psalms, 'Let his habitation become desolate, and let there be no one to live in it'; and 'His office let another take.' So one of the men who have accompanied us during all the time that the Lord Jesus went in and out among us, beginning from the baptism of John until the day when he was taken up from us — one of these men must become with us a witness to his resurrection." And they put forward two, Joseph called Barsabbas, who was surnamed Justus, and Matthias. And they prayed and said, "Lord, who knowest the hearts of all men, show which one of these two thou hast chosen to take the place in this ministry and apostleship from which Judas turned aside, to go to his own place." And they cast lots for them, and the lot fell on Matthias; and he was enrolled with the eleven apostles. (Acts 1:15-26)

Briefly pause.

Lord's Prayer

Leader: *St. Matthias*
Group: *Pray for us*

All make the *Sign of the Cross*.

Paul

(Chapter Sixteen)

Begin the session with the *Sign of the Cross* and the *Prayer to the Holy Spirit* (see page 10).

Excerpt from *The Apostles*:

From this, therefore, derive the greatness and nobility of the Church, that is, of all of us who are a part of her: from our being members of Christ, an extension as it were of his personal presence in the world. And from this, of course, stems our duty to truly live in conformity with Christ. . . . This is our definition: we belong among those who call on the Name of the Lord Jesus Christ. (pages 138, 140)

Quiet Reflection

NOTES

QUESTIONS FOR DISCUSSION

Questions for Study

1. How does Luke describe the early Christians? What identifies them?

2. How would you characterize Paul as a person and as a disciple?

3. What was at the center of Paul's faith (a) before and (b) after his conversion?

4. How would you describe Paul's conversion? What does his conversion reveal to us about the essence of Christian identity?

5. What were some of the difficulties Paul faced in his mission? What kept him going?

6. What are the two basic questions about faith asked and answered by Paul, both by word and by example?

7. What does "being justified" mean? What does the "new justice" consist of?

8. What are the two components of Christian identity according to Paul?

9. What is the role of the Holy Spirit in the Christian community according to Paul?

10. What do Jesus' words to Paul say about the relationship between Christ and the Church?

11. What characterized Paul's relationship with the Christian communities he established?

12. If the Church is the Body of Christ, what, according to Paul, does that mean for how the members of the Church should act and live?

Questions for Reflection

1. Luke describes the early Christians as those who "have risked their lives for the sake of Our Lord Jesus Christ." Does this definition still apply to modern disciples?

2. "How can one not thank the Lord for having given an Apostle of this stature?" (page 126). What about Paul are you grateful for? Who are the other Christians you have known or know about for whom you are particularly grateful?

3. Paul is the "greatest model of perseverance." In what parts of your faith journey has the model of Paul's perseverance as a disciple been helpful to you?

4. What does it mean to you to think of faith as Christ dwelling within you?

5. What concrete examples have you witnessed in which the identity of the Church as the Body of Christ has been very clear and powerful?

NOTES

CLOSING PRAYER

Scripture Reading

For if I preach the gospel, that gives me no ground for boasting. For necessity is laid upon me. Woe to me if I do not preach the gospel! For if I do this of my own will, I have a reward; but if not of my own will, I am entrusted with a commission. What then is my reward? Just this: that in my preaching I may make the gospel free of charge, not making full use of my right in the gospel. For though I am free from all men, I have made myself a slave to all, that I might win the more. (1 Corinthians 9:16-19)

Briefly pause.

Lord's Prayer

Leader: *St. Paul the Apostle*
Group: *Pray for us*

All make the *Sign of the Cross.*

Timothy, Titus, and Stephen

(Chapters Seventeen to Eighteen)

Begin the session with the *Sign of the Cross* and the *Prayer to the Holy Spirit* (see page 10).

Excerpt from *The Apostles*:

[Stephen] was one of the seven made responsible above all for charity. But it was impossible to separate charity and faith. Thus, with charity, he proclaimed the crucified Christ, to the point of accepting even martyrdom. This is the first lesson we can learn from the figure of St. Stephen: charity and the proclamation of faith always go hand in hand. (page 153)

Quiet Reflection

NOTES

QUESTIONS FOR DISCUSSION

Questions for Study

1. What was Timothy's role in Paul's mission?
2. What role did Titus play in the Early Church?
3. What problems was the Church in Jerusalem suffering at the time of Stephen?
4. What role did Stephen play in the Church in Jerusalem?
5. What does the laying on of hands mean?
6. Why was Stephen condemned by the Sanhedrin?
7. What was the focus of Stephen's discourse before his death?
8. How was Stephen's martyrdom similar to Jesus'?
9. In what ways was Saul's role in Stephen's martyrdom ultimately a bit ironic?

Questions for Reflection

1. None of the early Apostles or Christian missioners worked alone. Why is it hard to sometimes admit the need to work with others, even in a Christian setting? What must we die to in order to model our ways after Paul?
2. What are some possible consequences of separating faith and charity? How does such a separation impoverish both?
3. Stephen could have avoided martyrdom. Why didn't he?

NOTES

CLOSING PRAYER

Scripture Reading

I charge you in the presence of God and of Christ Jesus who is to judge the living and the dead, and by his appearing and his kingdom: preach the word, be urgent in season and out of season, convince, rebuke, and exhort, be unfail-

NOTES

ing in patience and in teaching. For the time is coming when people will not endure sound teaching, but having itching ears they will accumulate for themselves teachers to suit their own likings, and will turn away from listening to the truth and wander into myths. As for you, always be steady, endure suffering, do the work of an evangelist, fulfill your ministry. For I am already on the point of being sacrificed; the time of my departure has come. I have fought the good fight, I have finished the race, I have kept the faith. Henceforth there is laid up for me the crown of righteousness, which the Lord, the righteous judge, will award to me on that Day, and not only to me but also to all who have loved his appearing. Do your best to come to me soon. (2 Timothy 4:1-9)

Briefly pause.

Lord's Prayer

Leader: *Sts. Timothy, Titus, and Stephen*
Group: *Pray for us*

All make the *Sign of the Cross.*

Barnabas, Silas, and Apollos

(Chapter Nineteen)

Begin the session with the *Sign of the Cross* and the *Prayer to the Holy Spirit* (see page 10).

Excerpt from *The Apostles*:

Hence there are also disputes, disagreements and controversies among saints. And I find this very comforting, because we see that the saints have not "fallen from Heaven." They are people like us, who also have complicated problems.

Holiness does not consist in never having erred or sinned. Holiness increases the capacity for conversion, for repentance, for willingness to start again and, especially for reconciliation and forgiveness. . . . Consequently, it is not the fact that we have never erred but our capacity for reconciliation and forgiveness which makes us saints. And we can all learn this way of holiness. (page 157)

Quiet Reflection

NOTES

QUESTIONS FOR DISCUSSION

Questions for Study

1. Why are these three figures grouped together in this chapter? What do they have in common?
2. Who was Barnabas?
3. Over what issue did Paul and Barnabas disagree?
4. What role did Silas play in the history of early Christianity?
5. What was Apollos' connection to the Christian community at Corinth?
6. What complicated Apollos' time in Corinth?

NOTES

Questions for Reflection

1. We often tend to idealize the early Church, believing it spared of the problems we see today in the Church. Is such idealization justified? What were the general problems described in this chapter? What is the solution that emerges from the way that Paul and his collaborators dealt with the problems?

2. Paul and Baranbas disagreed, but then events came full circle. How do you reconcile after a disagreement? What role does Christ play in your reconciliation?

3. What is holiness?

NOTES

CLOSING PRAYER

Scripture Reading

But I, brethren, could not address you as spiritual men, but as men of the flesh, as babes in Christ. I fed you with milk, not solid food; for you were not ready for it; and even yet you are not ready, for you are still of the flesh. For while there is jealousy and strife among you, are you not of the flesh, and behaving like ordinary men? For when one says, "I belong to Paul," and another, "I belong to Apollos," are you not merely men? What then is Apollos? What is Paul? Servants through whom you believed, as the Lord assigned to each. I planted, Apollos watered, but God gave the growth. So neither he who plants nor he who waters is anything, but only God who gives the growth. He who plants and he who waters are equal, and each shall receive his wages according to his labor. For we are God's fellow workers; you are God's field, God's building. According to the commission of God given to me, like a skilled master builder I laid a foundation, and another man is building upon it. Let each man take care how he builds upon it. For no other foundation can any one lay than that which is laid, which is Jesus Christ. (1 Corinthians 3:1-11)

Briefly pause.

Lord's Prayer

Leader: *Sts. Barnabas, Silas, and Apollos*
Group: *Pray for us*

All make the *Sign of the Cross.*

Priscilla and Aquila and Women at the Service of the Gospel

(Chapters Twenty to Twenty-one)

Begin the session with the *Sign of the Cross* and the *Prayer to the Holy Spirit* (see page 10).

Excerpt from *The Apostles*:

A further lesson we cannot neglect to draw from their example: every home can transform itself into a little church. Not only in the sense that in them must reign the typical Christian love made of altruism and of reciprocal care, but still more in the sense that the whole of family life, based on faith, is called to revolve around the singular lordship of Jesus Christ. (page 167)

Quiet Reflection

NOTES

QUESTIONS FOR DISCUSSION

Questions for Study

1. Who were Priscilla and Aquila? What was their religious background, their profession? Where did they live?
2. What was their connection to Paul? How did they help him?
3. What was the importance of the "house church"?
4. How did the work of the Apostles and Christians like Priscilla and Aquila complement each other?
5. Who were some of the women important in Jesus' life and ministry?
6. What was the role of women during the Passion and Resurrection?
7. What theological basis does Paul give to the dignity of women?
8. Who were some of the women that Paul mentions in relationship to his mission?

NOTES

Questions for Reflection

1. What does it mean to say that a household can "transform itself into a little church"? In what ways have you experienced this in your spiritual journey in childhood or adulthood?

2. How do the roles of clergy and laity complement each other in the contemporary Church?

3. How have lay men and women been important to you in your own spiritual journey? What is your sense of how you can most faithfully serve Christ as a disciple working and living in the world?

NOTES

CLOSING PRAYER

Scripture Reading

I commend to you our sister Phoebe, a deaconess of the church at Cenchreae, that you may receive her in the Lord as befits the saints, and help her in whatever she may require from you, for she has been a helper of many and of myself as well. Greet Prisca and Aquila, my fellow workers in Christ Jesus, who risked their necks for my life, to whom not only I but also all the churches of the Gentiles give thanks; greet also the church in their house. Greet my beloved Epaenetus, who was the first convert in Asia for Christ. Greet Mary, who has worked hard among you. Greet Andronicus and Junias, my kinsmen and my fellow prisoners; they are men of note among the apostles, and they were in Christ before me. Greet Ampliatus, my beloved in the Lord. Greet Urbanus, our fellow worker in Christ, and my beloved Stachys. Greet Apelles, who is approved in Christ. Greet those who belong to the family of Aristobulus. Greet my kinsman Herodion. Greet those in the Lord who belong to the family of Narcissus. Greet those workers in the Lord, Tryphaena and Tryphosa. Greet the beloved Persis, who has worked hard in the Lord. Greet Rufus, eminent in the Lord, also his mother and mine. Greet Asyncritus, Phlegon, Hermes, Patrobas, Hermas, and the brethren who are with them. Greet Philologus, Julia, Nereus and his sister, and Olympas, and all the saints who are with them. Greet one another with a holy kiss. All the churches of Christ greet you. (Romans 16:1-16)

Briefly pause.

Lord's Prayer

Leader: *Sts. Priscilla and Aquila, and all holy men and women*
Group: *Pray for us*

All make the *Sign of the Cross.*

Jesus of Nazareth and the Church He Founded on the Apostles

(Chapters Three to Four)

Begin the session with the *Sign of the Cross* and the *Prayer to the Holy Spirit* (see page 10).

Excerpt from *The Apostles*:

Therefore, through the apostolic ministry it is Christ himself who reaches those who are called to the faith. The distance of the centuries is overcome and the Risen One offers himself alive and active for our sake, in the Church and in the world today.

This is our great joy. In the living river of Tradition, Christ is not 2,000 years away but is really present among us and gives us the Truth, he gives us the light that makes us live and find the way towards the future. (page 35)

Quiet Reflection

NOTES

QUESTIONS FOR DISCUSSION

Questions for Study

1. The Church that Jesus brought into being through the Apostles is marked by two kinds of universality. What are they?

2. Through what means can the Church today experience the "original communion" of the apostolic church?

3. What is "Tradition"?

4. What is the foundation of Tradition?

5. What holds Tradition safely across time?

6. Why is Tradition a gift?

7. In what sense are the Apostles the foundation of Tradition? What does Apostolic Tradition make possible?

8. What does the Apostolic mandate involve?

9. How does the Apostolic Tradition and ministry enable us to experience the Risen Lord today?

10. What are the roots of the word "bishop"?

11. How did the development of the Apostolic ministry safeguard the content and truth of the Gospel?

12. What is the essence of the role of the Bishop?

13. What did the second century theologian Irenaeus say about the importance of Rome?

14. "Through Apostolic Succession it is Christ who reaches us" (page 41). How does this happen? Why is it important?

NOTES

Questions for Reflection

1. Of the Apostles and other workers you have met during this study, have any emerged as particular favorites? People with whom you identify most closely? What about them inspires you or helps you deepen your faith?

2. In what ways can a reflection on Jesus' call and formation of the Apostles deepen our understanding of what Church is?

3. Why, 2000 years after the Apostles were called by Jesus, is their ministry a gift to us? What is it that the Apostolic ministry gives us?

NOTES

CLOSING PRAYER

Scripture Reading

Now the eleven disciples went to Galilee, to the mountain to which Jesus had directed them. And when they saw him they worshiped him; but some doubted. And Jesus came and said to them, "All authority in heaven and on earth has been given to me. Go therefore and make disciples of all nations, baptizing them in the name of the Father and of the Son and of the Holy Spirit, teaching them to observe all that I have commanded you; and lo, I am with you always, to the close of the age." (Matthew 28:16-20)

Briefly pause.

In this final session, it would be appropriate to pray the Apostles' Creed, slowly and with gratitude to God for the gifts and sacrifices of the Apostles:

I believe in God, the Father Almighty,
Creator of Heaven and earth;
and in Jesus Christ, His only Son, our Lord,
Who was conceived by the Holy Spirit,
born of the Virgin Mary,
suffered under Pontius Pilate,
was crucified, died, and was buried.
He descended to the dead;
the third day He rose again from the dead;
He ascended into heaven,
and sits at the right hand of God, the Father almighty;
from thence He shall come to judge the living and the dead.
I believe in the Holy Spirit,
the holy catholic Church,

the communion of saints,
the forgiveness of sins,
the resurrection of the body,
and life everlasting.
Amen.

Leader: *Holy Apostles of God*
Group: *Pray for us*

All make the *Sign of the Cross*.